The *ABCs* of Conscious Parenting:

Bringing Ease and Joy into Your Relationship With Your Child

By
Jill Mann Pekofsky

Published by
JLP Conscious Publishing

Jill Mann Pekofsky

DEDICATION

To my beloved children and husband, whose love and growth have empowered and encouraged me to be conscious in all my relationships. They taught me it was not only OK, but imperative, that we be authentic, mindful and intentional in all of our communication.

ACKNOWLEDGEMENTS

It is with the utmost gratitude and love that I acknowledge my daughters. First Leah, for her knowledge of words and how they go together and applying that knowledge so lovingly as my editor. Her grandmother would be SO proud!

And secondly my daughter Jenna, for her expertise in visual arts and creating the cover for the book, not just her technical knowledge but her vision of what I wanted and not letting me settle for just ok.

I am the most blessed mom on the planet. I love you both with all my heart.

And I must also acknowledge my husband, Larry, whose steadfast support was my rock, and has been for the last 26 years. I love you and know how blessed a wife I am as well.

"When a child hits a child, we call it aggression.
When a child hits an adult, we call it hostility.
When an adult hits an adult, we call it assault.
When an adult hits a child, we call it discipline."
— Haim G. Ginott

CONTENTS

INTRODUCTION

Are you wondering what exactly "conscious parenting" is? My husband, hoping to make a few million with this book, suggested I call it *50 Shades of Black and Blue: How to Raise Lumpy but Well-Behaved Children!* Well, the fact that you've opened this book means that *that* approach doesn't work for you. You have a desire to parent differently, so congratulations on your decision to be conscious about your parenting choices.

Conscious parenting simply means being aware of the impact that our words and actions have on our children and making an intentional or conscious decision to choose those words and actions mindfully. To me it means knowing that my parents did the best they could with what they had but that I have more tools at my disposal and want to parent differently from how I was parented. It means knowing that what I say and do *matters*.

WHO AM I?

I have a Master's in Parenting Administration from the Jill Pekofsky University of Parenting Hard Knocks! OK, not an officially accredited university, but I have been a parent for almost 25 years of two children. I've experienced diaper changes, teething, preschool, homework, bad test grades, science fair projects, PTA meetings, sleepovers, birthday parties, school dances, mean girls, sibling rivalry, puberty, having "the talk," ballet, gymnastics, endless sports practices, games, rehearsals, concerts and plays, parent-teacher conferences, first periods, first crushes, first jobs, navigating technology and social media and ... I'm still here. And more importantly, *they're* still here!

And even *more* importantly, my daughters, now 24 and 20, have grown into the confident, capable, loving young women that I had always hoped they'd become. I love spending time with them, and they love spending time with me. To hear them say they want to raise their kids just like they were raised is the most rewarding thing I could ever hope to hear. I wish the same for you.

So let me ask you:

Are you stressed out nearly every day and have no energy?

Are you feeling guilty a lot of the time and apologizing to everyone?

Are you questioning your parenting skills or your discipline strategies?

Are you wondering how in the world you're going to balance your work life and your family life or, if you're staying home, how you're not going to go crazy being with your kids 24/7?

Are you fighting with your kids all the time?

Are you arguing with your spouse about how

to raise the kids?

Are you just not happy?

Are any of these questions hitting home?

If so, let's think about these:

Do you want to gain confidence in your parenting skills?

How about being able to find that balance mentioned in the previous paragraph?

Do you want to let go of your need for perfection and eliminate mommy (or daddy) guilt forever?

How does it sound to be able to restore peace in your home and enjoy your children?

Would you like to wake up every day looking forward to being a parent?

If you answered yes to any of these questions, then join me in this journey into knowing, understanding and loving our kids — consciously.

Remember, we are responsible for our children's physical, emotional and spiritual well-being. It is our responsibility to guide, protect and teach children by modeling the positive expression of emotions. Responsibility can also be defined as the "ability to respond." Before we can respond, as opposed to react, there is a "space," and in that space we have the power — the responsibility — to make a choice. "Wait, do I want to go with my knee-jerk reaction, or do I want to take a moment to think about what would be the best action for both of us right now?" That is what conscious parenting is all about.

PREFACE

I married my husband in 1990. He is my third. My first was when I was 21. It was his second marriage and we tried to have children but were unsuccessful. He had two from a previous marriage. My second marriage was at 25, and he had had a child at 19 and then had a vasectomy and had no desire for any more. I basically gave up my lifetime dream of being a mother to be with this man, at the time the man of my dreams. When that marriage ended, I doubted I would ever marry again, but on the outside chance I did, I was certain it would be for one reason and one reason only: to have children. I could see no other point in going through all *that* again!

When I met my present husband, I was not looking for a relationship, let alone another marriage! But we started dating, and things started to click. We realized we had both been married before to people who already had children and couldn't have more. He had never really wanted kids, but as we started getting more serious we started talking about it, and he began thinking differently. We were both at a very different place in our lives. When we married I was 35, so as you can imagine, my biological clock was ticking, and loudly! So we decided to start trying right away. I became pregnant, the second month trying, with our daughter Leah. It was a wonderful and uneventful pregnancy. I absolutely adored being pregnant, partially because I hadn't thought it would ever happen but also because I was one of the lucky ones and had virtually no morning sickness and just felt great and so grateful. At the end of the pregnancy, I learned she was breech, which was the only negative to the whole experience. But once I got over not getting my "birth experience," she was born by C-section, healthy and beautiful. It all went very well. I nursed her successfully and just reveled in being a mom. She was a bright, articulate child, could count to 20 and say her ABCs by a year and a half, and was reading at a third-grade level at 3!

By the time she was 1 year old, I was thinking it was time for the second one, and as I wasn't getting any younger we decided to start trying. That was a very difficult time. We had two early miscarriages, and then a year during which we could not get pregnant. Finally, with the help of a fertility drug, we conceived again. After amniocentesis and learning we were expecting a healthy boy, I miscarried again and had to deliver my perfectly formed son, who was too young to survive. That was possibly the lowest point in my life. I'll never forget coming home from the hospital afterward and my beautiful 2½-year-old daughter hugging me and saying, "It's OK to be sad, Mommy." Wow! She'd really been listening to us validate her feelings!!

So then came the decision: If we try again, are we doing the same thing over and over and expecting different results (sometimes known as insanity) or are we persevering in the light of hardship (sometimes known as courage)? Well, I was determined to give our daughter a sibling and convinced my husband to give it one more try. After conceiving, then being put on strict bed rest from weeks 12 to 24, with a 3-year-old running around, our second daughter was born. She didn't breathe for what seemed like hours (probably about 10 seconds) but is now 20 and halfway through college. So, the moral of that story is it's a very fine line between insanity and bravery. I couldn't be more grateful that we gave it that one last try. Brave and crazy can be a powerful combination!

And so the journey of parenting two very bright, very precocious daughters began. This book is to help any parents facing this daunting task to do it with as much love, joy and presence as possible. It takes a lot of work to be a conscious parent. But having just gotten off the phone with my daughter — who said, "I'm liking this talking-every-day stuff!" – I can tell you it is so worth it!

I'm not going to go into that magnificent time of watching our daughters grow from defenseless little wiggling worms into walking, talking people. You know what that's like, and there are great resources out there for that time of life. I want to talk about those years after that, when they learn very quickly to yell "NO!" at the top of their lungs in the middle of the grocery store. Or throw themselves on the floor and have a full-blown tantrum. The times when you have to ask them again and again ... and again ... to do something they know is their responsibility but they just don't want to. Or when they ignore you altogether. Or, when they ask for something in that lovely, whining voice that sounds like fingernails on a chalkboard, over and over and over, after you've explained, cajoled, begged and finally yelled. Possibly, you've gotten so frustrated that you turned them around gave them a good, solid wallop on the bum! Those are the years I want to talk about. Those years that make you understand why some animals eat their young; those years that make you wonder how they're ever going to see their next birthday or how in the world you're going to survive the teen years! You know, *those* years.

My wish is that *The ABCs of Conscious Parenting* will bring you much ease and joy in your parenting journey.

Definition of "Conscious"

"Like a trained surgeon who is careful where he cuts, parents, too, need to become skilled in the use of words. Because words are like knives. They can inflict, if not physical, many painful emotional wounds."
– Haim G. Ginott, *Between Parent and Child: The Bestselling Classic That Revolutionized Parent-Child Communication*

Before we get into the tricks of the trade of conscious parenting, some discussion of the word "conscious" might be helpful.

There are many ideas out there about consciousness, or being conscious, but to start, here are some definitions from the Free Merriam-Webster Online Dictionary 2014:

Perceiving, apprehending, or noticing with a degree of controlled thought or observation 'conscious of having succeeded', 'we were conscious that someone was watching'.

Personally felt 'conscious guilt'.

Capable of or marked by thought, will, design or perception.

"Self-conscious."

Done or acting with critical awareness 'a conscious effort to do better'.

Being concerned or interested.

Marked by strong feelings or notions.

As conscious parents, we are aware and concerned with our parenting techniques. We are acting with critical awareness, marked by strong feeling about how our children react and behave with us and definitely how we react and behave with them. Awareness is simply making the unconscious conscious. Instead of reacting, we are being proactive in our words and behaviors.

Part of our being conscious in our parenting is being conscious of the baggage we carry into our parenting. And no matter how beautifully functional our upbringing was (and most of us would probably admit to some level of dysfunction!), we are *all* carrying some amount of baggage from our childhoods. In my house growing up, Dad ruled the roost, and Mom never rocked the boat. I grew up hearing her say things like, "Young ladies do not get angry" (think Mom might have been a bit repressed with her emotions?) and "Wait till your father gets home." And Dad was proud that he could control us with a look. You can imagine, then, the kind of baggage I grew up with. I didn't know exactly *how* I was going to prevent it, but I knew I did not want to inflict that kind of damage on my kids.

I am not going to get into a lot of psychology or theology in this book. I am not trained in either one. What I will say is if we deal with *our* baggage, we have a much better chance of giving our children less baggage to carry with them. And helping them to see that they are a part of something much bigger than themselves will also help us be more conscious and help them feel more empowered in their lives. There are going to be a lot of people throughout their lives trying to take their power away. As a conscious parent, we want to help them keep their power and still behave in a reasonably socially acceptable way. It's quite the balancing act! My intention with this book is to help you find that balance, enjoy your kids and your parenting, and help your children feel heard, valued, important and, most of all, loved.

Part 1:
The A's

CHAPTER 1

Attitude is Everything

> *"Parents often talk about the younger generation as if they didn't have anything to do with it."*
> – Haim G. Ganott

My husband is a numbers geek. I affectionately call him Mr. Spock because he can do the most amazing math in his head and figure out anything numerical. He shared this with me: When you assign numerical values to the letters in the word "attitude" according to their placement in the alphabet and add them together, they equal 100.

A=1
T=20
T=20
I=9
T=20
U=21
D=4
E=5

So the idea that attitude is 100 percent is not only a wonderful metaphor, it's an actual numerical fact!! Attitude is also primary and vital to conscious parenting. The attitude we take with our children is often communicated in much more than just the words we speak. It's in body language, tone of voice and facial expression, as well as words and actions. My husband used to think that since he wasn't yelling and screaming, he wasn't expressing anger. That couldn't have been further from the truth! If he was angry, you could feel it as soon as he entered the room: It just emanated from him! It was all in his attitude: silent, but screaming volumes. The same is true for all of us. People, especially our kids, pick up on our moods, our attitudes.

When we think about the teachers we had in childhood and what we remember about them, it's usually not what they taught us but how they made us feel. That is all about attitude. The way we feel around anyone is more about their attitude toward us, as well as our attitude toward them. Attitude conveys more about who we are and what we want or need than words ever could.

It's a wonderful practice as a conscious parent to check in with ourselves when we are not getting the behavior we want from our kids and to look at our own attitude at that moment. I know for myself, the more my kids acted out, the worse my attitude was, sometimes before and sometimes after. But my attitude was always in play.

QUOTES: SPEAKING OF ATTITUDE

When my kids were young, I used to watch parenting shows on TV, and they were fabulous. I want to tell you three of my favorite parenting quotes that I never wrote down but still remember because they impacted my parenting so strongly. The first is: "Parenting: The hardest job you'll ever love." Parenting might be the most important work we do on this planet. I can't think of another job that has more impact on our future than our job as parents. We are the single most impactful influence on our children — more than teachers, siblings, friends or society at large. We know we love our children. That goes without saying. But it's *how* we love them that makes all the difference and what conscious parenting is all about. And so the hard part comes when we realize that what I call "the knee-jerk method" isn't getting the results we want and that we have to start thinking about what we say and do. But, oh, how we will *love* the results! Hence, the hardest job we will ever love.

The second quote that really helped me in my parenting was, "You need to endure a little unhappiness to have a happy family." This was a major eye-opener for me. Having that history as a

4

people-pleaser, enduring unhappiness seemed to go against the grain completely. Everyone should be happy, pleasant and loving all the time! Well, you know how far that belief got me! In healing much of my own baggage, I learned that I grew up being shunned for feeling anything but happy. Remember, my mom used to say, "Young ladies do not get angry." So obviously, anger was not acceptable. And I had a tendency to cry easily and was teased for it. So now you're telling me I'm supposed to endure some unhappiness?? Well, I learned from experience that when I allowed my children to express their negative feelings in a positive way, the feelings dissipated and they went back to their sweet, fun selves. But only when those feelings were allowed, acknowledged and validated did that occur. That little statement turned out to be one of the most valuable things I could have learned as a parent. No one can feel happy all the time, and to expect my children to, or myself to for that matter, is a complete setup for resentment! So we endure the unhappiness by helping them feel all their feelings and letting them know that every feeling is just that, a feeling. And we do that by modeling appropriate expressions of anger, sadness or any other negative emotion. It needs to be acknowledged and validated, but it is not a fact and can be expressed appropriately.

The third, and perhaps favorite quote was this: "If it's not a problem for *you*, it's not a problem." This one gets very deep and requires us to not care what other people think of our parenting techniques. That can be so difficult, especially when your mother-in-law is watching you and criticizing and berating you as a parent, or even when a stranger on the street wants to tell you what you're doing wrong. This is where taking care of our own wounds from childhood and adult life becomes vitally important. The only way to stand firm in our parenting decisions in the midst of criticism is to have a reasonably healthy self-esteem. And my experience is that it comes from healing our own "stuff." I am not a therapist and cannot tell you how to do that. I can only tell you that for this parent, my healing was vital in giving my kids the best shot at growing up without the same challenges I had, because my parents didn't know any better. If you're reading this book, you know better. Do your work, so your kids have less of their own to do when they're adults. So this quote means standing firm in how you wish to parent your children. Trust your instincts. Trust what feels right to you, because if it feels right to you and you've done your work, it *is* right for you. And if someone else doesn't like it, well, that would be their problem, not yours.

SHAME

"Parental criticism is unhelpful. It creates anger and resentment. Even worse, children who are regularly criticized learn to condemn themselves and others. They learn to doubt their own worth and to belittle the value of others. They learn to suspect

> *people and to expect personal doom."*
> — Haim G. Ginott, *"Between Parent and*
> *Child: The Bestselling Classic That*
> *Revolutionized Parent-Child communication"*

Can you remember a time when someone said to you, "I'm so disappointed in you. What were you thinking?" Were those words helpful to you in any way? Did it help you to work through your actions and consider alternatives? It probably had the opposite effect: making you feel ashamed and inadequate. These are not the feelings we are hoping to instill in our children. We want them to feel empowered and capable.

Brené Brown, Ph.D., says, "Shame is the intensely painful experience of believing that we are flawed and therefore unworthy of love, acceptance and belonging. ... Shame can destroy lives." She also said, "Empathy is the antidote to shame. The two most powerful words when we're in struggle: me too."

Words such as "I'm disappointed in you" or "You know better than this," ideally meant to teach, do not create an empathetic connection or offer any assistance. They just point out a child's flaws. These statements used over and over create shame and the idea that we are bad, flawed, unacceptable and certainly unlovable.

Dr. Brown helps us distinguish between guilt and shame:

Guilt says: "I did something bad."
Shame says: "I am bad."

"Shame corrodes the very part of us that believes we can change," she says.

We use shame and blame often because it was used on us and it comes "naturally" for that reason. It takes conscious effort to use another way to achieve cooperation.

Some other shaming statements we may have heard or used are:

"I can't trust you anymore."
"What's wrong with you?"

"Why can't you just behave?" (Sometimes with "like your brother/sister.")

These statements create a sense of self-protection in our kids rather than a sense of self-regulation. Chances are we use them because we heard them. They are not necessarily what we want to say to achieve our desired outcome, but at that moment we don't have other choices in our arsenal.

We have to separate the behavior from the person. "I can't trust you" and "What's wrong with you?" say we are afraid this behavior is going to happen again and again. So instead of the shaming comment, let's share our real feelings: "It scares me that this is going to happen again." We can say we're disappointed in the outcome or the behavior (not the person) and we are scared this might happen again. Sharing our emotions with our child in a safe way allows him to feel like he can share his emotions because he feels safe, not shamed.

My hope is that as you read further, you will gain more tools and insights into eliminating shame, improve your own attitude with your kids and consequently improve the communication with them and cooperation from them.

CHAPTER 2

The 3 A's

*"Children become frustrated and resentful
when they view their parents as not
being interested in how they feel and in
their point of view."*
— Haim G. Ginott, *"Between Parent and
Child: The Bestselling Classic That
Revolutionized Parent-Child
Communication"*

There are three things all children want and
need, and I call them the "3 A's." They
are *attention*, *affection* and *acknowledgment*. Unwanted
behavior is a result of negative feelings, and not
getting any of the above three things will cause

bad feelings in our kids. If what we're looking for is a change in behavior from them, then we need to look at how they're feeling. And how they're feeling is often a direct result of not getting one of the 3 A's. So let's look at them one at a time.

ATTENTION

We've often heard that kids will try for any kind of attention, even negative attention if they're feeling like they're not getting enough of the good kind. So what do we mean by attention? Active listening is one kind. Really looking them in the eye, getting physically on their level and saying things like "Mmm hmmm, tell me more" are ways of active listening. Attention could be playing a game together, taking a walk together, doing most anything together. In our busy, busy lives, it's easy to get caught up in our day-to-day stuff and forget about simple attention. It is simple, it just isn't always easy.

AFFECTION

We all know what affection is, and it's another thing that can get lost in our busyness. A quick hug, a pat on the back, a kiss on the cheek all take seconds but can make an impact that can last a lifetime. It's up to us as the parents to consciously make the effort to be affectionate with our kids. Affection can be verbal as well. Telling them we love them, that we're proud of them, can go a long way in helping them feel good about themselves. This lets them know they are loved, and there may be nothing more important to them.

ACKNOWLEDGMENT

When we don't acknowledge our kids' achievements they feel unimportant, like they don't matter or are not worth our time or effort. Here's an example of a great way to acknowledge them.

You are on the computer on a very time-sensitive project. You need only a few more minutes to finish and your child comes up and really wants to show you the picture he's just colored. You are engrossed in what you are doing when he comes up and starts tugging on your arm, saying, "Daddy, Daddy, look at my picture, look at my picture!" What's your reaction? An unconscious reaction might be to give a cursory look and say, "That's very nice, honey." Then little Charlie goes, while tugging on your sleeve some more, "But Daddy, you didn't *really* look! Look at my picture! Look! Look!" After a couple more times of this, you might be likely to get very frustrated and raise your voice and say, "Can't you see I'm busy? You've got to let me finish this. Now go in the other room, and I'll talk to you in a few minutes." And out of the corner of your eye you see your son slink into the next room, or else he just yells, "I hate you!" and storms out. Sound familiar?

So, here's a suggestion. When he comes in the

16

first time, stop what you're doing, turn to face him, get right down to his level, look him in the eye and say, "Sweetheart, I *really* want to take a good look at your picture, but Daddy is in the middle of something and can't look right now. If you will give me 10 minutes [or whatever amount of time you need], then I will be done and can give you my undivided attention. Would you please go set the timer for 10 minutes and come tell me when it goes off? Then I am all yours!"

Here are the reasons this works so well:
1. He knows you've really heard him because you stopped and looked him right in the eye.
2. You've made a promise, and he knows you always keep your promises (right?).
3. You've empowered *him* to know exactly how much time to give you by setting the timer because they just don't get how long 10 minutes is, and somehow the inanimate, objective timer is a much more accessible timekeeper. You've eliminated the inevitable "Is it 10

minutes yet, is it 10 minutes yet?" over and over again. And *he* gets to tell *you* when the time is up. Then you have to keep your word. So be sure you give yourself more than enough time. Try it and watch what happens.

CHAPTER 3

Autonomy, Encouraging it in Your Child

So let's start with what is sometimes known as the "terrible twos." This is one of the most exciting times of your child's life because she is learning so fast and changing so much. She is curious about everything, and if she starts asking a lot of questions, you might find yourself in the dilemma we found ourselves in – offering an explanation for each question. We found, in some respects, we had created the proverbial monster. Our very bright, articulate daughter started demanding an explanation for *everything*! As a parent you know there are some things that are either beyond explanation, inappropriate to explain or just too time-consuming to explain right now.

Or you may find that no matter what you say or ask for, they respond with a resounding "NO!" One of the wonderful things we learned the hard way was that kids often feel powerless over their lives or surroundings but don't have the ability to let us know. We found that when we were able to encourage autonomy in their lives, they began to respond differently, and we heard "No" maybe a little less often.

CHOICE

Even by age of 2 or so, children can be given a choice, and it seems that choices help them feel in control of their environment. Asking them, "Would you like to wear the red pants or the blue today?" or "Would you like eggs or oatmeal for breakfast?" is enough of a choice for a child to feel empowered. We can even use this choice technique with our teenagers. When our 14-year-old son has not done his agreed-upon chore of taking out the trash, we can say, "So, Sam, would you like to take the trash out before

20

dinner or after?" It is very likely that even though you've so graciously given him a choice, you'll get pushback ("Oh my God, I can't *believe* you're bugging me about the trash *again*!" or something along those lines). We can just listen and say, "Yup, so what'll it be? Before or after?" and just keep asking, calmly, until he does it or answers. He will.

STRUGGLE

"Empathy, a parent's ability to understand what a child is feeling, is an important and valuable ingredient of child rearing."

– Haim G. Ginott, *Between Parent and Child: The Bestselling Classic That Revolutionized Parent-Child Communication*

One of the things that was so difficult for me in my early years of parenting was watching my child struggle. With anything. Or feel pain. Of any kind. That remains one of the hardest things about being a parent to this day! We want to protect our children from all of the harsh realities of the world. But if we look back at our own lives, and honestly think about our hardest struggles, we realize that those were the times of greatest learning and growth. So let's think about what we really want when we're struggling: We want someone to acknowledge that they see us struggling. We want to be able to voice our frustration and be understood. And we don't want someone to fix it for us! That is really the same with our kids, even though they don't know that's what they want. I've seen the difference in my children's response when I try to rescue them from their struggle and when I just acknowledge that I see them having a hard time. If I say something like, "Honey, why don't you do it this way" or just swoop in and do it for them, there is always resistance and often that makes their frustration grow ("Ugh! I can never do *anything* right!"). When I say something like, "Wow, I can see that you are really having a hard time with that" or "That looks really difficult," just that much acknowledgment can help ease their frustration. Then we can offer, "You let me know if you want some help with that." When we show respect for our children's struggles, they feel empowered. When we show them we believe that they have the ability to solve their problem, they tend to believe it too. I think one of the most empowering statements we can ever make to our children of any age is: "I believe you have everything you need inside you to solve this problem." And with the younger ones we can add, "And if you would like some help, just let me know."

Another thing that I later realized was a difficulty was the tendency to give them the answers to their questions immediately. They really have an innate ability to find the answers that they need on their own, but we often don't give them the opportunity to do that, because we jump right in with the almighty parental wisdom. It is another empowering act to, when they ask a question, respond with "That's an excellent question. What do you think?" That question says, "I believe you have the ability to figure this one out" or simply "I believe in you." What would we have given to have our parents believe in us? This is one of the most powerful, affirming, tools we can use as a conscious parent.

Another way to help them find the answers on their own is to suggest that they look outside the home for the solution. When Sara is doing a report on fleas and how they affect the animals we love, suggest that she call the local veterinarian for answers. "Mom, what kind of medicine do they give to dogs to keep them from getting fleas?" "That's an excellent question, Sara. Let's call Dr. Smith and see what he says."

One of the surest ways to help our kids be autonomous is to validate their feelings, which we will talk about in more detail later. As mentioned before, unwanted behavior comes from negative feelings. Children come into this world knowing very clearly how to get their needs met: by screaming. We reinforce that behavior by feeding them, changing them or just playing goo goo, ga ga with them when they scream. They scream; we give them attention. Our job as they grow is to help them learn that there are other ways to get their needs met, and save our ears and their vocal chords. Validating their feelings ("Wow, you are really angry!") will go a long way toward that goal.

Part II:
The B's

CHAPTER 1

Behavior — Ours

"Children are like wet cement. Whatever falls on them makes an impression."
– Haim G. Ganott

I imagine one of the reasons you are reading this book is that you want to change the behavior you are getting from your child. I know I was rather desperate at one point of my kids' childhoods to do exactly that! I started doing a lot of reading to get some help. I want to share with you some of the books I read that really made a difference in my behavior, which consequently impacted my children's behavior.

But before we get there, let's address our own behavior. One of the biggest and easiest traps for us as parents is that insatiable desire to be the perfect parent. It shows up in a myriad of ways. And one of the worst ways is feeling that if our child is in pain of any kind, we've failed as parents. We *hate* to see our kids in pain. There are few things that are harder for us to accept than that they need to experience some pain to grow. I don't mean we need to beat them to teach them. On the contrary: Life will issue enough beatings for them to learn from. We do not need to add to them. I believe our job as parents is to help them cope with the pain life dishes out in the healthiest way possible. We need to show them that we've had the same pains they are having and survived — and not only survived, but thrived. And we need to be that soft place for them to land. I told my kids over and over that they could always come to me with their problems. But I had to

28

back that up by not getting angry or freaking out when they did. If we want them to keep their word, we have to keep ours.

Remember in the "A's" chapter the TV quotes I talked about? One is "You have to endure some unhappiness in order to have a happy family." That quote speaks to this issue, that everyone struggles, has pain, is unhappy from time to time, and that it's totally normal and says to our child that I will be here for you when you go through it. Pain and struggle are a part of life, and the sooner they learn that they have what they need within them to get through them, the better off they'll be. And of course reminding your children that we will always support them through those times *and* that it's OK (and sometimes imperative) to ask for help, will help them too.

And then there are the times when we mess up. You know what I'm talking about. The time they did something that we had that knee-jerk reaction to, and we yelled or berated them before we knew it was out of our mouths. Or they

29

shared a feeling that we said, "Oh you don't really feel that way" or something like that. Then we went to bed and kept going over and over it in our minds that we blew it with them. Here's the thing: Every time we say to ourselves, "I wish I hadn't said that" or "Why didn't I think to say ..." we automatically get another chance. Life with our kids is open-ended. There's always another opportunity — in an hour, a day, or a week — to go back and say, "I've been thinking about what you told me before, about those kids teasing you on the playground. And I didn't really get how hurt you were. I realize now how upsetting that must have been for you." Compassion is always appreciated, whether it comes sooner or later. It's never too late to tell our kids we made a mistake.

And here's the other thing: Apologizing to our kids teaches them that we, like they, are human and make mistakes. And that we, like they, can learn from them. This will stick with them and teach them the importance of taking responsibility for their own behavior, because we

30

did! And be aware, they are *constantly* watching what we do, and how we handle things, and will mimic that. The world will not come to an end if we admit we made a mistake. On the contrary: The world becomes a safer place in which to make mistakes.

Here's an example: I had the unfortunate habit of beating myself up when I made a mistake. One night I was in the kitchen preparing dinner and spilled something all over the floor and started berating myself for it. "Oh my gosh, I cannot believe I could be so freaking stupid! What was I thinking? I should have been more careful. ... What an idiot. ..." And my dear darling daughter pipes up from the dining room and says, "Gee, Mom, don't be so hard on yourself. You just made a mistake, that's all. No big deal." I had probably said those words to her a thousand times. She heard me. And she was able to have compassion for me. It was an amazing moment. These are the rewards of conscious parenting.

Another way perfectionism rears its ugly head

is by trying to be "Superparent." We try to be all things to our kids, and probably to the other people in our lives as well. And in trying to please everyone, we spend all our energy and don't have the energy for our kids when they need us. This drive for perfection often comes in the form of unrealistic expectations of ourselves. And it often spills over into unrealistic expectations of our kids. We see other kids doing *everything*! It looks to us like they are doing every sport, every extracurricular activity, getting straight A's and having perfect manners. Other parents are quick to brag about their "perfect" kids, and we wonder what we're doing wrong. Parents are constantly broadcasting on social media a barrage of how perfect their kids are. We had to learn the hard way in our house that our kids would completely melt down when they were overdoing it. We ended up limiting them to one extracurricular activity a semester, along with Girl Scouts, because more than that totally stressed them out. They did not like that decision at all. But I will tell you there were a lot fewer meltdowns when we adhered to that rule. They learned from that experience that sometimes you just can't do everything you want! We need to let go of what we think we "should" be doing or what they "should" be doing. It is so hard to keep in balance in a family, and it is such a necessity. We have to let go of all those "shoulds" and look at what really works for *our* family, not anyone else's. We need to strive for our level of balance, rather than what someone else sees as balanced. That is the beginning of letting go of that perfectionism.

A great way to assess whether we're overdoing it as parents and striving for perfection is to look at all the commitments we currently have. We expect so much of ourselves that we can tend to overcommit. We can take a moment to write down all the things we have commitments to — the kids, our spouse, our church, community, school, extended family — everything but our job. We can then ask the question "Is this commitment adding to our quality of life or taking away from it?" Be brutally honest in answering. That is the only way to get to the truth. Let's also ask, "Am I doing this just for the ego stroke? Am I looking for acceptance? Have I been guilted into it?" Stop and think hard about the answers to these questions. For me it was a sense that if I didn't do it, it wasn't going to get done, or at least it wasn't going to get done right! I needed to look hard at my motives for all I was doing when I was totally out of energy for my kids and family. When asked to volunteer for something, I had to learn to say, "I'll have to get back to you on that" or "I'll have to think about that," rather than my knee-jerk reaction to say yes. In one of my Conscious Parenting workshops, I recently learned from an attendee another response to use when I need to say no and just can't quite bring myself to say that simple little word. I can say, "That just is not going to work for me right now." I love that sentence. It's concise and to the point, without being rude or vague.

Don't forget this as well: "Let me think about it" is a *great* line to use with our kids when they want an answer to something we're not sure of. I've often said, when they would bug me and bug me about wanting an answer now, "Well, if I answer you now, the answer is no. If you let me think about it, there is a chance that answer could change." Sometimes that even worked!

GETTING TRIGGERED: A HIGHLY AROUSED, ANXIOUS STATE

"What do we say to a guest who forgets her umbrella? Do we run after her and say, 'What is the matter with you? Every time you come to visit you forget something. If it's not one thing it's another. Why can't you be like your sister? When she comes to visit, she knows how to behave. You're forty-four years old! Will you never learn? I'm not a slave to pick up after you! I bet you'd forget your head if it weren't attached to your shoulders.' ... That's not what we say to a guest. We say 'Here's your umbrella, Alice,' without adding 'scatterbrain.' Parents need to learn to

respond to their children as they do to guests."
– Haim G. Ginott, *Between Parent and Child: The Bestselling Classic That Revolutionized Parent-Child Communication*

You know those situations when someone says something or does something and you immediately feel a clenching in your chest or stomach, you may see red or feel great tension in your neck or head, and you want to yell, scream or punch? *That* is what "getting triggered" means. Something deep down inside you, probably from something in your childhood, has been awakened by the thing said or done, and your body automatically reacts as it did when it happened the first time. Our bodies have remarkable memories, especially for strongly negative emotions. These are memories we are often unaware of, until they get awakened.

So, now that you know about this, notice when you're getting triggered by your child and become aware of your feelings. This means taking

36

that magic pause before saying or doing anything. Let the feeling of being triggered be your indicator that it's time to do *nothing*! Then, try using sensory words to describe those feelings to yourself, taking note of the sensations in your body, and see if you can connect it to an unmet need or some emotional stress.

Ask yourself some questions: Am I getting triggered outside the family too? Do I have too much stress? Am I spending too much time trying to figure out why my kids are freaking out instead of why I'm getting triggered? See if you recognize the feeling and if it's happened before. Then, practice bringing your mind back to the present. Lastly, ask yourself how you want to respond to what's been said or done. It takes a lot of practice to overcome the habit of reacting. And that's what we'll be doing, practicing. And like anything we practice, we will not do it perfectly and sometimes we'll blow it altogether. But we will be teaching ourselves a new behavior. Be patient with yourself, as you would be with your child learning a new activity.

Become conscious in the moment. Observe your thoughts and feelings and breathe, notice what's going on around you and in you. Getting still allows us to see what's triggering us and why. I would sometimes put myself in timeout, saying, "If I respond to this now it's not going to be good, so I'll talk to you about this in a few minutes." Or even, "I am way too angry in this moment to talk to you about this, so I'm going into timeout, and then we'll discuss what just happened."

"The best predictor of how well your children grow to develop their self-regulatory skills is how well you manage your own dysregulation."

– Lori Petro, founder of TEACH Through Love

Hyder Zahed, Ph.D., says in his book, *Create Your Legacy: Four Portals to Living a Life of Love and Caring,* "School psychologists say that it's important not to have arguments or fights with our children in the morning before school, especially on the day of a big test. Such negative emotional situations interfere with the child's ability to concentrate and handle the stress of a demanding exam, consequently lowering the little one's academic performance. Next time we are tempted to frown, burst into anger, or show irritation, disappointment, or disapproval, let us keep quiet and save the conversation for a better time when we're no longer upset, and instead, *smile*! If necessary, say something like, 'We'll talk about this later when we're both feeling better.' The results will be amazing."

CHAPTER 2

Behavior — Theirs

Here we're going to talk about the surprising benefit of tantrums and why letting your child become unglued is one of the best decisions you can make.

Before age 5 or 6, kids have very little control over their emotions. If our reaction to their meltdowns can be low-key and nonthreatening, they will more quickly build their regulating skills. The key is to stay in control of *our* emotions while allowing them to fully feel theirs. We may need to set boundaries to keep everyone safe and unharmed, but our goal will be not to come unglued as they do. We may ask, "If I let them act this way, won't they always act this way?" The answer is no, because the healthy development of the brain requires a depth of feeling. As children feel deeply, their brains develop so that they are able to feel deeply without a tantrum.

And we really will not die of shame when they have a tantrum in public! No matter what those around us do or say.

Three benefits of letting your child have a full-blown tantrum:

1. Feeling our feelings makes them less intense. Validation makes our emotions less scary and creates connection.

2. Feeling our feelings builds connections in our relationships that influence behavior. When we do this for our kids, it makes home and our relationship the "safety net," where they can be their authentic selves, and then behave beautifully outside the home. That was my experience with my kids. I can't tell you how often I would hear from

parents of their friends how well they behaved in their home and what lovely manners they had. Then at home, when I would watch their heads spin all the way around, I wondered who the heck those parents were talking about!! But that's exactly what we want: well-behaved children outside the home and authentically feeling children inside the home. And if I allow her emotions in a safe, supportive environment, an additional benefit could be that she will be more likely to hear my advice and counsel.

3. Feeling our feelings shapes the architecture of our brain.

The following is taken from the *Evanston RoundTable* newspaper. In a Jan. 7, 2009, article, Larry Gavin wrote:

"The debate about whether a child's brain is shaped by genes or by experience is over. 'It's both. And the truth is in the interaction,' said neuroscientist Judy Cameron, a member of the National Scientific Council on the

Developing Child (NSCDC). ...

"These early experiences — whether nurturing toward positive growth or stressful to the point of being toxic — have 'an enormous impact' on how the brain's lower-level neural networks are connected or 'wired' together and become the building blocks for more advanced circuits. Thus, 'early experiences determine whether a child's developing brain architecture provides a strong or weak foundation for all future learning, behavior, and health,' say the NSCDC and the National Forum on Early Childhood Program Evaluation (NRECPE) in their Joint Report.

"While brain circuits shaped through early experiences retain 'plasticity' and 'may adapt their architecture, at least partially, to experience in adulthood,' later interventions are less effective, less efficient and more expensive 'than getting things right the first time,' says NSCDC."

What I glean from this report is that when our children are able to express their feelings, it greatly impacts how they will behave and grow. It also states how important it is that they get this when they are young instead of treating issues later in life. Physiology is impacted by emotions! What a glorious thing to know!

CHAPTER 3

Behavior — Stopping It

Then there are those times when we simply *must* stop their behavior, for a variety of reasons: danger, inappropriate location, in-laws. There are also things kids do that, as parents, we would really *like* them to stop doing. That could be the major reason you're reading this book. You know what they are, the whining, arguing, fighting, pouting, yelling ... each behavior by itself can be tolerable, but an afternoon of one after another after another and we're ready to ship them off to boarding school or at least to their grandparents! Just before that happened in my family, someone introduced me to the book *1-2-3 Magic* by Thomas W. Phelan, Ph.D. I was sick and tired of yelling at and explaining everything to my kids, and they still weren't stopping what I wanted them to stop. I would like to offer some insights from this book that really helped me change the direction of my kids' behavior by using their techniques to change *my* behavior! It really was magic!

Here are some ideas from the book that were incredibly helpful to me in understanding why this process worked.

"The two biggest mistakes that parents and teachers make in dealing with children are: Too Much Talking and Too Much Emotion." (Page 15)

"If you have a child who is doing something you don't like, get real upset about it on a regular basis and, sure enough, she'll repeat it for you." (Page 16)

"Many of us seem to think or have been taught that kids are really just little adults. This is a false assumption, and can lead to disciplines that simply don't work, or huge scenes that everyone feels terrible after. This idea, which is erroneous, can be called 'The Little Adult Assumption.'" (Page 11)

This assumption gives us the belief that kids are basically unselfish and reasonable, and are giving and honest — just littler versions of us. So if your kid is arguing with his brother, you just give him the Golden Rule, and good solid reasons why he should not argue with his brother, for example:

1. He will be happier.
2. He will grow up getting along with people, which is very important.
3. It is always better to settle things calmly rather than yelling and screaming.

And after explaining this so clearly and logically, he should just say, "Gee, Mom, I never thought of it that way. I probably wouldn't like that either. Thanks!" And immediately goes and plays nicely with his brother! Obviously, this doesn't happen very often in real life.

With this approach, we are relying heavily on words and reason in trying to get kids to change their behavior. And more often than not, words and reason fail miserably. And sometimes they will simply go in one ear and out the other. Then, in our frustration of trying words and reason over and over, we end up in the "talk-persuade-argue-yell-hit syndrome. " (Page 12)

49

THE 1-2-3 TECHNIQUE IN A NUTSHELL

Your 7-year-old is climbing on the kitchen counter to get into the cabinets. You come in and find him there and start to panic. Your first instinct is to yell at him because you've told him so many times not to climb on the counters, it's dangerous and he could get hurt. Your next idea is to grab him and fling him into his room for the rest of his life. You've had advice to ignore it, let him fall because he won't get hurt that badly, to spank the daylights out of him, or to take away everything he holds dear until he gets the message.

Since none of these seem to be acceptable solutions, here's what would happen with the 1-2-3 technique: You would hold up one finger and say, "That's 1."

It has no impact; he's still screaming. After a few seconds, you hold up two fingers and calmly but firmly say, "That's 2." Same reaction. A few more seconds and you hold up three fingers and say, "That's 3, take five." This means you have given him two chances to cool it, and he didn't, so he goes for timeout, or if you prefer "rest period."

He "does his time" (one minute per year of life).
When he comes out ("Time's up, Jimmy. You can
come out if you want") there is no explanation,
nothing said about the timeout, unless it's absolutely
necessary. You do not say, "Now are you going to be
a good boy? Your sister doesn't behave like that …
blah, blah, blah." That's using words again, trying for
understanding on his part. If more of the behavior
you want to stop occurs, you count it again.

*"The fact of the matter is, the power of the 1-2-3 does not
come so much from the time out itself; it comes from the
interruption of the child's activities."* (Page 28)

THE NO-TALKING AND
NO-EMOTIONS RULE

When we count and say, "That's 1," we turn the
responsibility of what happens next over to the child.
When we start talking after that 1, we take it back.
Chances are they will not stop their behavior until
you've given three or four good reasons why they
should, but that doesn't usually work anyway.
Another problem with all that talking and emotion is

that they cannot hear the warning "That's 1" when it's mushed up with all that other jabber.

You may have already tried counting with your kids, but I bet you had no idea that the talking and emotions were defeating your attempt. Here's an example from the book of how a scene could go when we take back the talking and emotions:

"That's 1. Come on now, I'm getting a little sick and tired of this. I don't know why you can't do just one little thing for me — LOOK AT ME WHEN I'M TALKING TO YOU! — when we're always doing everything for you. OK, that's 2! One more and you're history, young man. Do you really enjoy going to your room or do you just get a kick out of trying to drive me crazy?! (Pause for breath) OK! I'VE HAD IT! THAT'S 3! GET OUT OF MY SIGHT! I NEVER WANT TO SEE YOU AGAIN! EVER! TAKE FIVE! BEAT IT!" (Page 21)

The main problem with this scenario is that often, when they hear you getting upset, that's their signal that war has been declared. And they've probably won many times out of their sheer persistence and our exhaustion of patience. The "No-Talking, No-

Emotions Rule" takes all of those possibilities out of the picture.

"What's good about the 1-2-3? The 1-2-3 will save you a lot of breath — and a lot of aggravation. Parents and teachers say it makes discipline a whole lot less exhausting. You give one explanation if absolutely necessary: 'Timmy, climbing on the cabinets is dangerous. Please get down now,' and then you count if he argues and does not get down. There is no extra talking and no extra emotion. You stay calmer and you feel better when you get a good response at 1 or 2. Also, your authority with the 1-2-3 is not negotiable. One more reason the 1-2-3 works so well is that the punishment is short and sweet; about 1 minute per year of the child's life." (Page 25)

Here's an example of how I used the 1-2-3 with one of my children. We were out to dinner with my in-laws one evening and we were waiting outside the restaurant for our table on a summer night. Near us was a railing that was the perfect height for climbing. Of course my youngest, about 4 or 5 at the time, did just that. I told my daughter, in a very reasonable tone, to get down from the railing, that it was not for climbing on, it was for keeping people out of the garden. She promptly ignored me. So I said it again, a little more strongly, to which I got whining, arguing and fussing in return. At this point, my mother-in-law started observing the situation, and I could see the judgment all over her face! So I said it one more time, sharply, loudly, to no avail — and then I remembered: 1-2-3! I said calmly, "That's 1. Please get down." And she got down. No argument, no fussing, just did it. Magic. Pure and simple!

There is so much more information in this book. There are explicit instructions on how to have a "Kickoff Conversation" with your children, what to do when your child won't go into timeout, and encouraging wanted behavior.

I can't encourage you enough to get the book or video of *1-2-3 Magic* and start using it right away. But only if you want to eliminate yelling, arguing and whining.

Part III:
The C's

CHAPTER 1

Communication

COMMUNICATION

Why kids talk back and what to do about it

If behavior is communication — what is it saying? We tend to assume back talk means "I don't respect you" or "I don't have to listen to you," but it's really saying, "I want you to hear me, see me, listen to me." It's a plea for connection with you. Somehow we need to do this in a way other than: "I know you're frustrated, but you can't ..." or "I know you're upset, but you have to ..." No matter what flies out of her mouth, what her back talk is really communicating is how she feels, her ability or inability to self-regulate without you, and the state of your relationship. What if we were able to say, "Wow, I don't know where that came from, but I definitely want to know more?" That could acknowledge that we see that they are just not able to speak as clearly without our help as they would be with our help. If we can offer help instead of criticism, or reaction, offer to really hear what they have to say, then their sassiness can be dissipated. We can say, "I don't like it when I'm spoken to in that way, but I'm very curious about what's upsetting you." This statement sets a clear boundary while taking a real interest in what's up with them, and that interest in turn helps them not feel that the only way to get our attention is in a negative way.

Josh Shipp, teen parenting expert and former troubled teen himself, had this to say about back talk and what it means:

"Imagine you're on a roller coaster. You

sit down in the seat and the first thing that happens is some guy comes around and sort of pushes down that lap safety bar, secures the lap safety bar. Now if you're like me, what's the first thing you do? You grab that bar and you push it, you pull it, you wiggle it, you test it. Now think about it — do you push and pull and wiggle that bar hoping that it will give, hoping it will fail, leading to your inevitable death as you splash to the pavement? Of course not. You push it and you prod it and you test it hoping, confirming, it will hold.

"Listen to me, that teen in your life is doing the exact same thing. They are pushing you, prodding you, testing you, hoping, confirming, you will hold. I mean, at a time in their lives when so many things are uncertain, they need to know that you are certain. At a time in their lives when so many things are unstable, they need to know that you are stable. And, at a time in their lives when so many things are erratic, they need to know that you are consistent.

"So good news! If the teen in your life pushes you, it doesn't mean that you are a bad person, an imbecile, or doing it all wrong, or messing things up, or saying the wrong things! It simply means you're dealing with a teenager."

A pitfall I found myself in was wanting to know everything about their day. I had girls, who were much more forthcoming with information than boys tend to be, or so my friends with sons told me. So I would ask a myriad of questions, thinking I was showing interest in them, but it tended to cause them to just roll their eyes, and shut up. It became clear, after many difficult afternoons, that they would share what they wanted to share, when they wanted to, and not what I wanted to hear when I wanted to hear it. My questions would have the opposite effect I was looking for. They'd offer one-word answers or just say nothing. Somehow with kids, it seems that the more questions we ask, the fewer they want to answer. I found that often a simple "Welcome home. Would love to hear about your day if you feel like talking about it" gave them the knowledge that I cared about what happened with them, but that I also cared about their space and energy. I was not demanding that I get what I wanted, which was a full report. Plus, it left the door open, so that if there was something they wanted to talk about but weren't ready to, they could always bring it up later.

You may have noticed in your parenting that when kids express their negative feelings they don't usually say, "Gee, Mom, when Grandma told me to be quiet and speak when spoken to, I didn't care for that and hope she doesn't say that again." They usually say, or scream, "I *hate* Grandma!" And what do we say? "You do not hate Grandma, and I don't ever want to hear you say that again" or "You're just saying that because you're tired" or "There's no reason to be so upset" or something along those lines, denying their feelings. These reactions of ours are knee-jerk parenting. Our kids say something that triggers something deep inside us and we react. Then they react. And we usually end up with a screaming match that leaves everyone feeling awful.

In this instance, giving their feelings a name can help them calm just a bit and give you a chance to take that vital pause before responding. That could sound something like "Wow, you sound furious!" So often they will reply with "Yeah, she's so mean" or "She shouldn't have said that" or something that will take it down a notch. Then there is room to possibly ask for more about that. And just the act of not shutting them down, but *acknowledging* their feelings, they feel heard. And when you take it one step further and validate their feelings by saying, "You know, it makes sense that you feel that way," that can be one of the most empowering things we can say to them, or anyone. They will feel heard and accepted, even when how they're behaving is not their best. The surest way to exacerbate the situation is to tell them they are wrong to feel the way they do. Feelings are never wrong, they are just feelings. Facts can be wrong or right, but feelings simply need to be expressed, and then accepted by the listener. The surest way to ease intense feelings of anger or hurt is to validate them.

If your kids stay really mad or upset, one of the best tools I've ever been shown is to ask them to draw how they feel. "You know, I hear how angry you are. Can you show me in a picture just how mad you feel?" There is nothing like drawing to get those feelings out, calm down and feel understood and accepted, even when they're at their ugliest. That was one of the greatest discoveries in parenting: letting my kids know that *all* feelings are OK. It's how we express them that makes all the difference. I grew up feeling that anger was unacceptable, especially from me, so I was always afraid of anger, mine or yours. No one ever told me it was a natural thing to feel angry or that there might be a way to get my anger out without hurting someone else. Drawing their feelings gives children an appropriate way to deal with those intense and sometimes scary feelings of anger. Because I wasn't allowed to get angry, I spent most of my childhood, and much of my adult life, stuffing my anger. And we all know that anger turned inward becomes depression. Been there, done that.

3 magic words for managing difficult behavior

Then there are the times when they ask the same question over and over even though they know the answer is no. They've asked, we've said no. Again and again. Then they may begin with the one-word question: "Why?" And how likely are we to get frustrated and answer, "Because I said so!" Maybe they need to get a little clarity on why it's no.

There are three magic words that I've learned can stop the question: "Tell me more."

These three words can be used instead of no in so many situations. "Tell me more about why you want a pony." They might just need to fantasize. Or maybe they just need some new coping strategies in the moment. With these magic words you can learn all sorts of things that are going on in their heads or their world. "Tell me more about why you have to go over to Jimmy's house *right now*?" There's a good chance your child needs support and doesn't know how to ask for it. She doesn't want us to explain the reason we say no or to fix the problem. She wants to be heard, validated, and then to have us work through the problem together.

"Kids don't need us to fix them or solve their problems — they want us to stay calm and steady as they learn to ride the waves. Play. Say yes. Be curious."
— Lori Petro, TEACH Through Love

"Tell me more" gives your child the opportunity to go deeper into why they want what they continue to ask for. It can also give us the space to calm down and not react. It's kind of like when we give them their wishes in fantasy.

I just want to pause for a minute to say, this act of validating feelings is something we can use not only with our children, but also with anyone who comes to us with a problem. When I think about what I really want when I share a problem, it's just to be heard and perhaps understood. And one of the most satisfying ways to feel heard is to have my feelings validated. That's not the same as having a complaint about someone and having another join in on the complaint and turning the discussion into a character assassination session. It doesn't have anything to do with the person (or situation) we are upset about. It just says, I get where you are, what you are feeling about this. And that is what true listening is. It's a gift we give to someone when we truly listen and don't try to fix or add to the fire. It is a gift we as conscious parents give our children that will pay them dividends for a lifetime.

One of my most satisfying moments as a parent was overhearing my daughter, talking to a friend on the phone, say, "Wow. That must have been really awful. It makes perfect sense you feel that way." I think she was 12 at the time! At 20 now and a resident assistant in her dorm at college, her residents constantly tell her how understanding she is and how they feel so safe coming to her with a problem. That, fellow parents, is one of the fabulous benefits of validating your child's feelings!

As has been mentioned, there is a direct connection between the way children feel and the way they behave. Unwanted behavior, more often than not, stems from negative feelings. One way to help the behavior is to validate those feelings, especially the ones that cause them pain or upset. How do we help them to feel better? We accept their feelings — all of them — and give them outlets for expressing them. Their behavior is their communication. What are they trying to tell us with their behavior? Here are some scenarios where we might find ourselves in knee-jerk parenting mode and some suggestions for a more conscious response. Remember, *we need that pause* to respond responsibly.

CHAPTER 2

Cooperation

COOPERATION

One of my favorite parenting books that I read and utilized when my kids were young was *How to Talk So Kids Will Listen & Listen So Kids Will Talk* by Adele Faber and Elaine Mazlish. This book is filled with scenarios, illustrations and ideas that in a page or two can give you tools to use right then and there. I loved that it didn't require me to sit down and read the whole book before it helped. I would like to share one of the exercises from that book, or my take on the exercise.

Here's a scenario:

Your daughter comes out of the bathroom having just had a shower and promptly drops the soaking wet towel on your bed. You've had numerous discussions with her about this and asked her more than once to not do that. And there that wet towel lies, soaking through your bedclothes.

What I might have done in this instance is gotten extremely frustrated and started yelling, "Oh my gosh, how many times have I told you not to put your wet towel on my bed?? You know how much I hate that ... blah, blah, blah." I'd have gotten myself all worked up and probably upset her as well, when I might have saved myself a lot of heartache with one of these skills. There are five of them offered, because some will work with some kids some of the time, and others will work with other kids other times. Or some will work one time but not the next, so you try another.

1. Describe what you see or describe the problem.

"There's a wet towel on my bed!"

When I simply describe what I see, I take the blame, anger and accusation out of the statement, and somehow she can hear it when it's free of those

intense emotions. Actually, all of these skills do just that.

2. Give information.

"The towel is getting my bed wet"

Just a slightly different way of doing the same thing, so if she doesn't hear the first, she might hear the next.

3. Say it with a word.

"The towel!"

This one worked so well in our house. We had a basket by the front door that was for book bags, and the girls were to drop their book bags into it instead of the middle of the living room floor. It slid in and out from under the table by the door. They didn't even have to pull it out, as it invariably sat pulled out, which was fine. They would then proceed to come home and drop their book bags on the floor in front of the basket. You can imagine the things I would start screaming ... until I tried this skill. One of them would walk in, drop her bag in front of the basket and head to the kitchen. I would loudly say, "Book bag!" and she would immediately go back, drop it in the basket, no argument, no pouting, just done. It was a miracle!

4. Talk about your feelings (briefly!).

"I don't like sleeping in a wet bed!"

This one, rather than giving information on what has happened, gives information on how you feel. Not what they did, not how frustrated and aggravated you are with them, but how you feel about the issue at hand. Much different than how you feel about them. Much less loaded and much more effective.

5. Write a note.

This is one of my favorites. You place the note above the towel rack that says:

"Dear _____,

Please put me back so I can dry.

Thanks!

Your towel"

This works so well in scenarios in which you have asked over and over and they just seem to forget. And kids do forget. They really are not doing it to get us upset (most of the time). This is a great way to remind them without nagging and enables them to be responsible without having to be reminded verbally by us. Like the inanimate timer in a previous scenario, the inanimate note does the work!

A note can also be a great way to bring up issues that are difficult or touchy. It has a number of advantages over sitting down to a discussion, which can intimidate the heck out of your kid, or just bringing it up in the moment of upset. First, it enables you to think about exactly what you

73

want to say before you say it and without all the emotion. And second, it gives your child time to digest the difficult thing you wanted them to hear. They do not have to respond immediately. They can get upset privately if necessary before talking about it and can think about what *they* want to say without just reacting to what you have said. It is a win-win way to prepare for a possibly emotion-filled conversation.

Notes can be used on all kinds of issues, as can all of these techniques. But here's an excerpt from the *book How to Talk So Kids Will Listen* (Pages 88-89):

"People have asked us, 'If I use these skills appropriately, will my children always respond?' Our answer is: We would hope not! Children aren't robots. Besides, our purpose is not to set forth a series of techniques to manipulate behavior so that children always respond.

"Our purpose is to speak to what is best in

our children — their intelligence, their initiative, their sense of responsibility, their sense of humor, their ability to be sensitive to the needs of others.

"We want to put an end to talk that wounds the spirit and search out the language that nourishes self-esteem. We want to create an emotional climate that encourages children to cooperate because they care about us.

"We want to demonstrate the kind of respectful communication that we hope our children will use with us — now, during their adolescent years, and, ultimately, as our adult friends."

This has happened with my amazing young adult children, and I cannot begin to express my joy and satisfaction with how our relationship continues to grow and improve.

CHAPTER 3

Correction, & Praise

Alternatives to punishment

"Misbehavior and punishment are not opposites that cancel each other — on the contrary they breed and reinforce each other."

– Haim G. Ginott

Many parents will want to know what to do when the above skills have not worked and our kids have done something we strongly oppose or something they've been told not to do. There are many alternatives to spanking, timeout (other than in the *1-2-3 Magic* context), taking something away, and other forms of punishment that just don't seem to "fit the crime." Wouldn't it make more sense to have natural consequences for their actions? Here's one possible way, again from *How to Talk So Kids Will Listen & Listen So Kids Will Talk* that we might use to help our kids navigate this world of confusion.

The scenario goes like this. Your son has taken your saw from your toolbox without asking and has left it out in the rain, and now it is covered with rust. You are furious and ready to take away everything he loves and lock him in his room for the next five years! Here are some suggestions, other than those, that might bring effective change.

    1. Express your feelings strongly, without attacking character.

"I'm furious that my new saw was left outside in the rain to rust!"

With this statement, I am being abundantly clear about how I feel, but I have not screamed at my son for being stupid and inconsiderate, even though I might think he has been both. We can all hear what's said to us much better when our character is not being attacked.

2. State your expectations.

"I expect my tools to be returned when borrowed."

OK, now he knows what you expect if he is going to have the privilege of using your tools.

3. Show him how to make amends.

"What this saw needs is a little steel wool and a lot of elbow grease!"

Feel free to tell him where to find the steel wool. You may also need to define "elbow grease"!

4. Offer a choice.

"You can borrow my tools and return them or you can give up the privilege of using them. You decide."

What I love about this step is that it puts the decision totally on the child. This causes him to stop and think about what he really wants and what the consequences are of not thinking. Helping your child think and reason things out can go a long way when he is faced with much more dangerous choices, especially in the teenage years.

5. Take action.
Child: "Why is the toolbox locked?"
You: "You tell me."

Again, we are giving our child the opportunity to think and figure things out on his own. We are not abandoning them to their own misery, but we remain available to explain, if needed. This question makes him think about what he's done and the natural consequences that follow.

6. Problem solving (possibly my favorite parenting skill).

Step 1. Talk about the child's feelings and needs. Let your child know that you understand that he sometimes forgets to return things and that it can be hard to remember.

Step 2. Talk about your feelings and needs. Then, let him know that even though that's true, you need to keep your things in working order and to have them returned in the same condition as when they were borrowed.

Step 3. Brainstorm together to find a solution you can both agree to.

Step 4. Write down every idea you both have, without evaluating, and don't exclude *any* ideas, no matter how absurd they may seem.

Step 5. Decide together which ideas you will keep, which you will cross out, and which you can both follow through on.

Step 6 (optional). Write a contract and both sign.

This problem-solving process is so respectful and honors *both* parties' needs and wants. In the step where you write down ideas, it's important that no ideas are judged by either one, each idea is accepted and written down, not necessarily to be implemented. You then have the process of eliminating ideas that don't work for one or the other. A compromise is almost always reached that both of you can agree on. This way, the child has had input in his own "punishment," because sometimes there has to be a consequence.

5 Common Parenting Mistakes That Can Turn Conflict Into Chaos

It is our perception of our child's reaction that fuels our anger and patterns of punitive discipline.

Comparing or judging our parenting styles and labeling ourselves too permissive or too authoritarian doesn't help us to become more conscious about our emotions and reactions. It just makes us feel bad about ourselves. Instead of a label or a judgment, ask yourself, "What is my probable parenting response?"

Yelling (intimidating, dominating, scaring).

Explaining (trying to convince, legitimize, rationalize, wanting kids to quietly accept).

Negotiating ("If you do this, then you can do that," one more minute turns into 30, teaches them comebacks, back-talking, arguing).

Resisting (shutting down, refusing to listen based on their tone or behavior; we do it when we feel disrespected).

Giving or giving in (patronizing, distracting from the emotion or conflict, indulging in order to stop the behavior).

Here are some examples of what to look at if any or all of these patterns of behavior fit our parenting styles:

Yellers: Knee-jerk reacting.
1. Track what triggers you — can you see patterns?
2. Become aware: Notice what behaviors in your child trigger certain behaviors in you.

3. Meet your own needs for self-care first! This is so vitally important for a conscious parent! Just as the flight attendant tells us that if the oxygen masks drop, put ours on before we help someone else with theirs. Make sure that when you find yourself reacting or overreacting, look to your self-care and what might be missing there.

Explainers: Our kids are not having a thinking problem, they are stuck in an emotion.

1. Stop talking — what's needed here is active listening.
2. Regulate yourself — Pay attention to how you're feeling and if agitated, revert to Step 1.
3. Let kids have their feelings! This is the validation piece. If they are stuck in an emotion, their way out is for us to recognize it, name it, validate it, and allow their healthy expression of it. They may need our guidance to find the healthy expression.

Negotiators: Think compromise will get you what you want.

1. Get emotional. Think empathy! Again, an opportunity for validating.
2. Listen for feelings — another reminder that we need to stop talking.
3. Connect using your right brain. Negotiators use logic, explanation and lots of words. Remember the too much talking discussion from *1-2-3 Magic*? Validation of feelings is what's needed.

Resisters: Removing yourself gives them the power.

1. Allow emotions — at the risk of repeating, validate!
2. Hold boundaries — kids don't want limits, but they desperately *need* them!!
3. Stay close — they need us to help them sort it out.

Givers: Can't stand to see them hurting.

1. Be OK when they aren't, sit with emotions.
2. Don't fix.

3. Maintain safety and connection.

I can't stress enough the vital importance of our own self-care in order to be aware of the things we do that *don't* work.

Praise

"If you want your children to improve, let them overhear the nice things you say about them to others."

– Haim G. Ginott, Ph.D.

I always thought that praising my children was vital to their self-esteem. How else are they going to know how marvelous and wonderful they are? I grew up feeling like no one ever praised me and consequently had low self-esteem. But what I've learned in my experience and research is that simply saying "You're wonderful" or "That picture is lovely" can sometimes have the reverse effect of what we were going for.

If you think about praise you have heard in

your life, this might make sense. Imagine you are going to an important business meeting and you change out of your sweatpants into your suit. You get to the meeting and your colleague says, "You are always such a sharp dresser!" What might your first thought be? Think about that. Or you just found out you were having unexpected dinner guests and threw a quick dinner together out of cans and frozen food, and your guest says, "What a great cook you are!" What might your thoughts be about that praise? If you think about your answers to these questions, it might make sense that just telling your child how "good" she is or how "pretty" a picture she drew might give them similar reactions. The first praise you got about your clothing might have elicited a thought like "Well, you should have seen me an hour ago!" And the second might have caused you to react with "If you think I'm a great cook based on this meal, you have pretty low standards!" And even though your kids may not have the sophisticated thought processes to give them these reactions to your praise, the feelings will be the same. They will feel like you are either lying or you didn't pay attention.

But if your colleague had said to you something like "I know you found out about this meeting at the last minute and you still look completely put together!" you might feel proud because he was paying attention to your situation and telling you what he sees. And if the dinner guest had said, "Wow! What a creative meal to have put together on such short notice!" then you might feel appreciated for your creativity and not necessarily be feeling like you have been fed empty compliments.

Our kids feel the same things. So in conscious parenting, praise might sound more like this: "Wow, look at that picture! I see big red squiggles and dark brown lines! You really put some effort into this drawing!" You are acknowledging what they did and paying attention to what you see, and they feel seen and valued. Not just blown off with an offhand "It's lovely, dear."

Another way of praising in a way that makes them feel valued is to put a word to what they've done. For example, if Janie has finished some really hard homework that she didn't want to do, rather than saying, "Nice work, honey," we might say, "Well, Janie, you really struggled with some of those problems, and you didn't want to do them, but you toughed through it and now you're done. That's what I call *perseverance*!" Not only do they feel like you really appreciate what they've done, you've also given them a new word they can add to their vocabulary because you've used it in a context they understand.

When I did that with my daughters, I could see their chests puff up with pride at this big powerful word I had used to describe them. And invariably I would hear that word come back out of their mouths down the road. Win-win.

How to Talk So Kids Will Listen describes praise and self-esteem in this way:

Instead of evaluating ("Good" ... "Great" ... "Fantastic!"), describe.

> 1. Describe what you see.
>   "I see a clean floor, a smooth bed and books neatly lined up on the shelf."
> 2. Describe what you feel.
>   "It's a pleasure to walk into this room!"
> 3. Sum up the child's praiseworthy behavior with a word.
>   "You sorted out Legos, cars and farm animals, and put them in separate boxes. That's what I call *organization*!"

We know from our own experience that the world is not so quick to praise but is very quick to criticize. When we can change that tendency in our homes, it gives our kids a fighting chance to not take the critics of the world to heart. We are responsible, as parents, for giving our kids the best possible opportunity to feel good about themselves, and when they feel good about themselves they are more likely to cooperate, communicate and cohabitate in ways that are pleasant and effective. And isn't that our goal as conscious parents?

CONCLUSION

And so, it is my wish for you that the tools offered in this book bring joy and ease into your relationship with your child. There are no magic tricks, no perfect words, no guarantees in parenting. There is only you and your child, and how you communicate.

They are going to push you to your very limit.

They are going to aggravate you and challenge you and force you to be a more patient, tolerant person. Or they will trigger you to be a more reactionary person. Both will happen.

The goal in conscious parenting, as in life I think, is to use the tools offered here more often and more quickly, and react to being triggered less often. These tools will help us react less. They will not stop us from being triggered. They will simply give us that gift of pause, thought and choice in our responses. We are always at choice as to how to handle any situation in parenting or life in general. For me the question was "OK, I have a choice. But how the heck do I make the better choice?"

These tools that I learned, and offer to you with love, were the answer for me. I hope they give you what they have given me: magnificent relationships with my young adult daughters. They still trigger me. They still aggravate me (as I do them!). But they also give me more joy, pride and love than I ever thought was possible in my life. And that, my fellow parents, is what conscious parenting is all about!

BIBLIOGRAPHY

Between Parent and Child: The Bestselling Classic That Revolutionized Parent-Child Communication
By Haim G. Ginott, H. Wallace Goddard, Alice Ginott
Published July 22, 2003, by Harmony (first published 1965)

Create Your Legacy: Four Portals to Living a Life of Love and Caring
By Hyder Zahed, Ph.D.
Published Nov. 1, 2013, by Balboa Press

How to Talk So Kids Will Listen & Listen So Kids Will Talk
By Adele Faber and Elaine Mazlish
Published in 1980 by arrangement with Rawson, Wade Publishers Inc.

1-2-3 Magic: Effective Discipline for Children 2–12
By Thomas W. Phelan
Published Jan. 28, 1995, by Parentmagic Inc.

Helping Adults Understand Teens & Teens
Understand Themselves
http://joshshipp.com
Josh Shipp

Parenting With Love and Logic
By Foster Cline and Jim Fay
Published in 1990 by NavPress Publishing
TEACH Through Love, http://www.teach-through-love.com
Lori Petro

Made in the USA
Columbia, SC
11 April 2018